IN THAILAND IT IS NIGHT

In Thailand
It Is Night

Poems by
Ira Sukrungruang

University of Tampa Press

Cover illustration by J. R. Miller

Manufactured in the United States of America
Printed on acid-free paper -
First Edition

The University of Tampa Press
401 West Kennedy Boulevard
Tampa, FL 33606

ISBN 978-159732-105-1 (hbk.)
ISBN 978-159732-106-8 (pbk.)

Browse & order online at
http://utpress.ut.edu

Library of Congress Cataloging-in-Publication Data

Sukrungruang, Ira.
   In Thailand it is night : poems / by Ira Sukrungruang. -- First edition.
      pages cm
   ISBN 978-1-59732-105-1 (hbk. : alk. paper) -- ISBN 978-1-59732-106-8 (pbk. :
alk. paper)
   I. Title.
   PS3619.U38915 2013
   811'.6--dc23   2013002829

Contents

GARUDA

    An Attempt to Explain Reincarnation • 3
    Ancestors • 4
    Bird Dreaming • 6
    Drawing Buddha • 7
    When Peacocks Scream • 10
    The Country I Never Had • 11
    Fortune • 14
    Impossible Things • 15

PHRA NARAI

    Fathers, Princes All • 19
    Ill Man Bowling Alley • 21
    My Father's Life In Six Stanzas • 22
    Karma • 28
    Third World Dogs • 30
    Plans for the Next Life • 33
    Sestina • 34

NANG UMA-DEVI

    After the First Snow • 41
    Altitude Sickness • 42
    Where Is the Winter Storm . . . • 43
    How To Tell Your Mother . . . • 50
    Crossing the River Kwai • 51
    Vacations • 52
    On the Phone We Say Only Happy Things • 53
    Beautiful Sadness • 57
    The World Drowns Atlas • 58
    Because the World Is Cluttered • 60
    Into the Keeping of Men • 61
    In Thailand It Is Night • 62

HANUMAN

What I Want to Remember in the Next Life • 67

Acknowledgments • 71
About the Author • 73
About the Book • 75

Garuda

(Bird Creature of Buddhist Mythology)

An Attempt to Explain Reincarnation

You've got to be a bird to understand any of this . . .
—Dean Young, "Centrifuge"

. . . and you've got to be the meadow to understand dusk,
and the growing grass to know yearning, and the heart to know waning light.

You've got to be the immigrant's son to understand tobacco fingers,
lying to women of other shades, and the versatility of rice.

You've got to be the emptiness between stars to know how deep
the cracks in the sidewalks are, and a Midwesterner to know the taste of soil

and the August heat that scorches the rubber off shoes and that the space
between stars is less mysterious than a pasture.

You've got to be a dog to understand the beauty of the bunny's
zig-zag trail through the snowy yard, the joy of the sound

of rattling keys within a lock, and the exquisite relief of scratching off a tick.
You've got to be born a turtle to understand time.

You've got to travel to another country to understand
when words have no meaning and the waters are threatening and

the only bridge is carried by a fluttering multicolored insect.
You've got to watch the gecko scurry across Buddha's hand

and the moss growing on his nose,
and you've got to laugh, you've got to let the world know

you are trying to wake the unwakeable.
You've got to die happily, just once, to remember all your lives.

Ancestors

I have met some of you—I'm sure—
                              in this life.

The blue jay, for example, knocking in a thicket of dead wood,
and did not wing away when I approached. It disclosed
some essential message in code.
Was that you, Grandfather, warning me of the ravine
I would stumble down soon, the fall leaves underneath
me like a wooden sled?

And later, a squirrel plummeting from a hickory,
            plummeting with a resounding thud,
                              plummeting
in the path of my sneaker and scurrying away.
I backed off.
Noticed the camouflaged frog on the trail, throat
bubbling with insect. Was that you who fell, Great Aunt,
wise woman who rushed to relay
the invasion of Japanese soldiers? And you,
Great Uncle, teaching me
the importance of looking down?

The sun, magnified by noon,
spotlighted two gulls
                  kiting
                              the sky over an Iowan lake,
and I wondered whether I was witnessing
a forbidden love story: two lovers—one rich, one poor—
            bisecting the air,
                  carving currents,
            interwoven,
                  interlocked,

[4]

braided and spiraling,
from one life
to the next and the next,
and in each I was there, too, though I am certain in one
I was a quivering leaf that observed everything.

Bird Dreaming

I'm trying to understand this new place—where the rhythms of the land are not in sync with mine. The sounds, the sights, the feel—so strange. I wonder if this is what the astronauts felt when they landed on the moon, this sense of displacement, this otherworldly impression. But the birds— they have me spinning. Where are the robins and their pretty songs? Where is the iridescent glow of the indigo bunting? The gold finches like jewels in flight? Here the birds are long-legged and wild looking, like the heat and oppressive humidity. Here they stand in medians of busy highways, surrounded by endless strip malls, a new jungle.

I dream of birds not from this world, colors screaming as loud as their calls: fantails with checkerboard heads, sibias with lightning-streaked breasts, bulbuls with crowns of metallic gold. They flit in the Florida flat, pose on top of the tallest strand of waving grass, dance in a whirl of kaleidoscopic color until they disappear and I wake up. I tell a friend about the dream, and she says I must be in a good place in my life, that birds symbolize happiness. She's a new friend, so I don't ask her why I squeezed my eyes shut so hard they began to tear just to get back to the wind in my imagined world.

Drawing Buddha

1

So that every morning I wake and ſtart with a pencil
and a ſtill hand. Secrets are kept

2

in quiet, between dark and light,
between breath, between thought and aċtion.

3

Move across the page, delicately, as if tracing the inside

4

 of a lover's thigh or caressing a dog's silky head.

5

Start with meditating hands because the hands hold
suffering. Be sure to curve the fingers
and palms, and be sure the curve cups karma,
or a splashing sparrow, or a sleeping cat.

6

Hands lead to arms, arms to shoulders, shoulders to
neck, neck
to face.

7

Pout the lips, plump them effeminate.

8

Then the eyes; so much has been made of the eyes. Wide open,
the world is translucent. Half, we queſtion waking life. Closed,
what dreams circulate
the mind? Think hard,
but do not ſtill your hand.

9

Sometimes decisions are made within the body.

10

Remember, the torso should look like this:
\ /

11

and the legs, which are crossed and covered
in robes—sketch creases, wrinkles,
folds like a map of rivers and mountains.

12

What is left is the top
of the head. Capture a plummeting comet
or ice cream dropped from a great height.

13

When finished,
begin again.
Begin.

When Peacocks Scream

They suddenly appeared,
the two of them,
in suburbia, Chicago, in the hot of the summer.

Two peacocks
in the middle of a soccer field
housed in a cage that looks out only to the east.

Monks fed them
carrots and lettuce,
grown in the temple garden.

They screamed
when the trucks rumbled out of the truck yard,
blaring on their horns.

They screamed
when Thai children banged
on the cage with insistent fists.

They screamed
at night, monks running, robes half on, hoping
their racist neighbors hadn't killed them.

When they fanned open,
only when the day was quiet, they danced around each other,
a tango of blue and green.

The two of them,
forever huddled close on a mound
of hay, necks entwined, waiting for the sun to rise,

but never able to see it set.

The Country I Never Had

—*after James Wright*

1

What was it he said: The dark wheat listens?
To what? Time that begins to dry stalks
and drop apples from bruising heights?

The cranes that land and take flight
in a cornfield, their bodies
like arrows pointing somewhere?

To the darkening sky, perhaps, and the reddening
moon, to the heat that sizzles even at
night and the cicadas that sing the end of summer?

The crows have gathered. Their black wings are spread
over something we do not see.

2

The short woman hums
a song from the morning dream
she forgot she dreamt.

The tune is familiar. It is solemn like the first drops of rain
on a dirt road.

3

Please, look above you.
Up there. Be still.
That leaf is singing its goodbye.

4

I would like to get to the house
in the diſtance,
the one with
the porch light on.
The night is heavy
like a winter quilt.
If I lie down,
I'm afraid I will be swallowed . . .

Fortune

I don't know
how we arrived
here,
but I know
there are finches
flying through
windows
without glass,
singing the blue
out of the sky,
and that is all right
with me,
one way or another.
My palms are up.
I want you to read.

Impossible Things

When pigs devour the moon and cows fly, their udders
raining milk on the world, when dogs and cats
lick each others paws inſtead of plummeting to the earth,
when inside a small town girl
is a metropolitan skyscraper with a viewing deck,
when one ant runs away
from the colony because he feels underappreciated,
when the pawn turns king and fucks
the queen out of spite while the knight watches
on his wooden horse and the bishop crosses himself, when
revenge is served lukewarm like Spanish gazpacho with a side
of grilled cheese and milk from the flying cow, when the rock
is not dumb or ſtuck in a hard place but flying toward a window,
when a penny earned is ſtill
a measly penny, when man's beſt friend is a cheetah that eats
the slow dog, when a friend in need is ſtoned to death,

the fly on the window with its many eyes
will ſtill buzz assuredly around the ſtink
left behind and it will see juſt how impossible
the task we have before us is and it will think,
for the love of god, ſtrike
me down with that swatter
please.

PHRA NARAI

(Creator and destroyer of all living things)

Fathers, Princes All

A friend tells me
her daughter believes her father
is Prince Charming
on horseback, sweeping
her away to a spired-castle.
She wonders why she isn't
a Princess,
why she is more the witch
who boils children,
why the father is bestowed
royal praise?
What I don't tell her is true
stories never end
with a kiss, but begin with one,
and birds don't sing
melodic songs but drop
droppings on cars,
and talking animals
sometimes end
up on the blacktop.
Time will make the prince
consider legacy. He will mount
his steed and find another quest,
better than the first, even if
he has to cross oceans
to start again.
He will age, Prince Charming,
not well either,
because now he finds
himself shrunk,
and his chiseled chin
sags like the rest of him.

I won't mention
long nights yearning
under the moon
or his sad howls
with baying hounds.
Eventually, the prince will forget
he is a prince, will forget
many things, and find himself
a man with mortality
nipping at his heels.
In the end, I say,
it is the witch who wins,
the wicked witch
made
Queen.

Ill Man Bowling Alley

It is really El Mar,
but my mother sees the pink neon
and the flashing bulbs around
looping cursive letters
and reads *Ill Man*,
like my father
when he rages
because the toothpaſte is spent,
banging those callused
chemiſt hands on the countertop,
waking me from a six-year-old's dream
to find him speaking
in that harsh foreign tongue,
words I was taught never to use
no matter how mad I got,
and my father raising the toothbrush
like it was a machete,
shaking it violently at my mother
who says, seek help,
I-bah, *you insane baſtard*,
it's only toothpaſte.

And when we bowl,
my mother seems to forget
about my father in her ſtep and release
because someone who bowls as beautifully
as she does can't possibly have that toothpaſte image
in her mind
as she hooks the ball from right to left,
and it rolls and rolls
with that smooth rumble,
rolls with that sole intent of knocking everything over.

My Father's Life in Six Stanzas

Before you were what you are now,
you were a boy without a father,
rough-elbowed and wild, who learned to swim
because your mother threw you in piranha waters.
You lived outdoors most of the time,
killed snakes and grilled them for dinner.
Once a boa twined around your legs
while you slept, and you slit it open,
only to release squiggling baby snakes. No wonder
you refused to go in the reptile house at Brookfield Zoo.

Before you were what you are now,
you were a young man full of dreams,
five inches taller then, lieutenant in the Thai air force,
base boxing champion, expert with a ping-pong paddle.
You had a mole on your chin that made you sexy
to the women you often visited,
though you already had a daughter named *Nu Laik*, Little Mouse.
You bragged to your military buddies
that America was in your sights,
and the women there should watch out
because you were going to woo them all
with the Thunderbird you planned to buy.

Before you were what you are now,
you were a tile factory worker off Pulaski Avenue,
alongside blacks, Poles, and southside Irish.
You learned to talk tough
because in America you began to shrink.
You found a woman. You liked her mouth
and married her in Chinatown in 1974.
Two weeks before the Bicentennial,
your son was born, and you loved
his dense black hair, his telling eyes—parts of you.
You were near legend to him:
the man who killed a boa,
the man who swam with piranhas.

Before you were what you are now,
you were a wayward man who found another woman,
your son's best friend's mother,
face like a Chinese porcelain doll—
white and fragile.
You came home from work later and later,
knowing nothing of how your son waited for you
until his eyes could no longer stay open.
And when the woman with the beautiful mouth
shouted things that stung your pride,
you thought that mouth was not so beautiful anymore.

Before you were what you are now,
you were a man who ran away from everything—
the boy who loved you,
the woman with the now toothless mouth,
your son's beſt friend's mother.
Back in Thailand, you told people's fortunes and
worked in an office of women,
not satisfied with your life,
never satisfied.
When you wanted to come back,
even America rejeſted you.
Failing the citizenship teſt,
you were a decade behind in your answers,
Reagan no longer president.

Now, when you call the boy who once loved you,
you wonder why he answers impatiently.
You say you'll be in the country awhile,
working again. You don't tell him where, a secret.
He finds you at McDonalds
sees how small you've become.
There are things on your tongue you want to say,
soft things, things that mend.
The fryer beeps for your attention,
and the boy waits, patiently, crisp bills in hand,
as the line behind him coils like a snake.

Karma

My father's friend has taught his mynah to say *I owan*, Hey, fatty!
He, not the bird, looks like a gigolo, his indigo shirt unbuttoned
to the divot in the middle of his chest, shirt rolled up to the elbows
in 80s-style cuffs. He has a hairy mole on his cheek. He clucks to the mynah.
He says he rescued the mynah after it flew into his helmet as he steered
his motorcycle through dusty roads. He turned the motorcycle around;
the mynah limped about, its left wing stuck open. The Buddhist in him
cradled the squawking bird in one hand, while navigating busy Chiang Mai
streets. When he got home, he tried to bend the wing back, but
    he couldn't.
He tells me the mynah knows other words:
        soi, beautiful, *sawasdee*, goodbye, *bah*, crazy.

I say: Soi.
The bird says: I owan.
I say: Sawasdee.
The bird says: I owan.
I say: Bah.
The bird says: I owan.

My father's friend laughs. The black mynah hops along a thin wood plank,
streaks of yellow around its eyes like detailed flames on a hot rod.
Handing me a dead cricket, my father's friend says to bribe it—
lunch for friendship, an offer the mynah cannot refuse. I stick the cricket
through the slit in the cage. The mynah hops to it, squawks, exposing its
    bell
tongue. The mynah snatches the cricket from my fingers; I hold onto
thin black legs like eyelashes. Definitely now, I am the mynah's friend
    forever,
both of us understanding the power and importance of a meal. I can see it

in the mynah's eyes. My father's friend sweeps a trail of red ants off the
    marble
porch. He says I should try the other words again:

                 soi, beautiful, *sawasdee*, goodbye, *bah*, crazy.

I say: Soi.
The bird says: I owan.
I say: Sawasdee.
The bird says: I owan.
I say: Bah.
The bird says: I owan.

My father's friend acts stern with the mynah, though I can see the laugh
forming on his lips, the way the corners of his mouth twitch.
He cannot contain himself. He puts a dead cricket in between his lips.
He slides open the door to the cage and reaches in with both hands,
    cupping
the mynah gently. He speaks mumbled words I don't understand. The
    mynah
takes the cricket, and my father's friend cleans whatever is left with his
    tongue.
It is a strange kiss. After my father's friend places the mynah back in the
    cage,
I notice the twisted wing, bent inside out. I am fat, I say, but you are
    broken.
My father's friend places a protective blanket over the cage. Scowls. The
    mynah
understands, he says. Through the fabric he whispers:

                 you are beautiful; the boy is crazy; goodbye.

Third World Dogs

1

After the blizzard, I dig
trails for my dogs, canyons branching
into canyons.
From the porch, they are mice in a maze,
the snow walls dwarfing their cocker bodies.
They follow their noses to dead ends.
The only true path leads to a dog door and into the house.

2

Father fingered missing
patches of leg beside his right knee.
Mah bah, he said. Mad dog.

Mother, patting my cockers,
knuckles the tops of their heads. She ſtretches
her entire arm, keeping
them at a diſtance.

This is the Thai way: caution before love.

Josh Capca asked if I ate dogs.
I told him no,
but the rumor spread.

3

A young man in overalls shovels snow off my roof.
The dogs bark at the scraping sound above them.
They hide between my legs, in the dark
space underneath my desk. I wonder
if they think the world is ending.

I remember a dog in Thailand—middle
of traffic—cars, mopeds, *tuk tuks* speeding
by, spouting black clouds.

The dog owned the road.
It had a dirty color,
pointed ears,
a ribbed body.
It lifted its back leg and licked.

Plans for the Next Life

Bangkok nights are easier on the dog. Gone is the scorching sun, the flies and gnats that hover around his eyes, the tropical humidity that weighs oppressively on his joints. A dog's life is not simple in this Buddhist country.

This dog is lucky. He does not traverse busy intersections, does not have ticks hanging off his jowls like pimples ready to burst, does not beg for scraps. He eats his master's leftovers—stewed pork leg, Peking duck, steamed fish heads—luxuries no Thai dog could ever imagine. He fears nothing, not even thunderstorms during the monsoon season that rattles the foundation of the house, not even the rat that trespasses in and out of the hole in the kitchen. This dog sleeps on the smooth marble porch, and is bathed weekly in shampoo more expensive than his master's servant girl, which she remarks on daily. Every evening, this dog lies next to his master, the night sky above them, hazed in pollution and city lights. His master covers him with the same blankets he arrived in fifteen years ago—washed and pressed daily—and the dog falls asleep to his master's whispering mantra. *In the next life, my blessed friend, I hope we meet in friendlier climates.*

Sestina

1

Begin
with a joke
about the yellow
man who crossed the road
and the chicken that stood
in devouring grass.

2

My father cut grass
every weekend. Before he began
he ſtood
above the mower, contemplating. Teens played a joke
on our lawn, bleaching it. For some reason, our road
was always filled with cars on Sundays, yellow

ones that reflected the yellow
sun, and as my father mowed, the mower spit dead grass
and rock againſt car doors, leaving dents. Afterward, the road
was filled with yard detritus, upswept, carried off by wind. Begin
with a joke
about a yellow man who mowed a dead lawn till he could hardly ſtand.

3

What ſtood
in my way was Cowardice, yellow
and large like a ſtar. My friends joked,
high on grass,
about my eyes, slits, the weight of weed beginning
to make the metaphorical road

fuzzy. I forgot where we were or what car I rode
in. What ſtood
in my way was the mountain I was beginning
to climb, because I was yellow
too, like the grass
my father cut, like my father, and the joke

about the chicken is the joke
about the yellow man, crossing the road
towards the devouring grass,
hoping to find safety. What ſtands
in front of you, father and son, are more roads, and yellow
road signs. Where do you begin?

4

The grass was not a joke
we wanted to remember. Forgetting is difficult. Begin with a road
and a man standing with the belief that the yellow line will lead
somewhere.

NANG UMA-DEVI

(Mother Goddess)

After the First Snow

Here, metaphors slip off the tongue,
 sarcasm a second language.

There, the body speaks
 vulnerability.

Here, silences shatter eardrums.

There, old men hobble,
 live beyond numbers,
revered like saffron-robed monks.

I was born
 under a half moon over Lake Michigan,
 in a hospital that monitors vitals.

My mother dreams
of endless fragrant fields of rice
and her clairvoyant father
waving her back home.

It gets cold here,
 the snow floating and sticking to the spruce,
 weighing down its limbs
 like fat underneath the arm.

There the sun sizzles skin,
the equator splits the peninsula.

We whisper a secret.

A stone Buddha waits on a mountain
for a sparrow to nest in the cavity of his ear.

Altitude Sickness

This night, my heart beats in my ears
and toes, pulsating in fingertips
and temples, explosions
in my body. Meanwhile, cranes
land in some distant Illinois field,
cardinals wing by like blown kisses, and the dogs
of the world lie under a sycamore large enough to shade them all.

Earlier, the housesitter left a message
that everything is fine; the cockers
are being over fed and my mother called twice,
leaving the first message in English, the second
in Thai.

Sleep comes slow tonight because the darkness
is loud and has much to say. A moth flutters
against the window screen without the siren
of light. What darkness
does it seek, this moth, what cracks and caves,
what loneliness does it wish to fly into?
I open the window,
let it flutter in.
Tell me about longing,
how it wounds like an arrow.

Where Is the Winter Storm that Blew a Turkey into Our Birch?

1

It was a shock
to see him perched
on a bowing
limb as the wind
tousled his feathers.
He must have thought
himself as small
as the finches
that pecked the niger
seeds from the tube feeder.
From our window
we watched him
through the obscuring snow,
like fuzzy reception
on a bad television,
and we wondered what
he would eat
when the ground was
buried under so much
white . . . .

2

The storm has skirted
the lake shore,
carried its weighty
clouds to an elsewhere
where the land
is green and soft
and waiting for
a steady flurry
to kiss the ground.
Younger, I looked up
and thought this was what
salt looked like
from the vantage of food.
I closed my eyes.
I didn't want them
to dissolve
from the heat
of my cheeks and lips and tongue.
Listen, my friend,
I've been waiting
all winter to be breathless,
waiting for you
to wash out the world
and leave it white
as an unwritten page.

3

There are places
in the world where
snow is a myth.
Yes, they say,
the earth crumbles
and drifts down
in white flakes. Yes,
they say, the world
eats itself.

4

Is it snowing there?
my mother asks first thing.
She is countries
away. She sounds
close. Where she is
the dogs seek shade.
How much? she wants
to know. Does it look like
the pictures you sent?
Today, she says,
it is hot here. So hot.
Later she will ask
again about the snow.
She will ask me what it looks
like where I am.

5

And so it is word upon word
upon word.
What accumulates
is the thick, cold
blanket of a life.
And in that
there are memories
of diving deep
and not drowning,
of diving again
and staying under.

6

The cardinal looks like
a splash of blood. It pecks
at fallen seeds.
When it flies
away, what remains
in my vision
is blush on snow.

7

. . . and so my wife
grabbed gloves full
of sunflower seeds,
which she tossed
into the storm,
at the foot
of the birch. He darted
across the yard and into
the woods, disappearing
behind fallen hickories.

How To Tell Your Mother There Will Be No Grandkids In Her Future

Don't enter conversations
about generations. Use the art
of misdirection. Tell her the rain
is falling. Tell her today
you saw a cardinal,
her favorite bird, and it was
feeding its young seeds.
No. Better not mention
the young. Tell her,
instead, the garden is coming in
thick this spring,
and the tulips have multiplied,
their buds like hands in prayer.
Better yet,
tell her about the work
crying in your briefcase.
Tell her you wish
you had three lives:
one for work, one for your dreams,
and one for her. That one
will have as many Siamese warriors
as she wants, swinging on a tree
as wide as an ocean,
its limbs twisting and turning.
In that life,
they listen, those warriors,
for the sound of her voice.
They wait for her to emerge
from the jeweled temple.

Crossing the River Kwai

The bridge vibrates minutes before the train arrives. I avoid
the space between the wooden slats.

My steps creak. The rusted handrail undulates
like a wave. Can you see them? my mother says.

Ahead, she eats fried bananas from a paper bag.
They are everywhere. Grease coats her lips and fingertips.

They are the ones in memory
when bombs fell in the village over,

rattling the tin roof. Soldiers' footsteps
like tigers prowling. There's one, she says, her finger sharp.

He has yellow hair.
In the place she points, there is nothing

but wild vines creeping up lush tropical trees.
The train's horn splits the air. It spews out soot. We step

on to a ledge that looks west. As the train passes,
an arms-length away, my mother waves at everyone,

and everyone waves back, except for a boy who stares at us
like we are the cause of all his troubles.

When it becomes a dot, my mother makes it to
the other side. She talks to the trees.

He says where he is
the sun is blue and the water is on fire.

Vacations

The highway ſtretched, and in between
feeding Dad grapes, you turned from the front seat
and tried to ease my boredom with ſtories. I liked
your talk. Dad said little.
He pointed out a Jaguar, a Benz, a Porsche.

When we moved off the interſtate, we passed a funeral
procession, a long line of headlights
in the afternoon. We put our hands together—
even Dad for a bit before returning
to the ſteering wheel—and you said,
We are born, we grow, we die.

Once, after you told me my ears used to be the size of beans,
there were lights in the diſtance and without word, we put our hands
together, only to bless
a line of Harleys, whose engines roared
like an apocalyptic ſtorm. Nothing
could contain your laughter—not even
when Dad rolled up the window—which was so loud,
I wondered if you'd wake the dead.

On the Phone We Say Only Happy Things

1

These legs are too short to step over a crack
let alone an ocean,
and our voices cannot bridge miles, cannot
say what needs to be said

2

because language is no longer
sufficient, because understanding is lost

3

in distance and night and day.

4

When you rise,
I fall, and vice versa.

5

Yesterday, home fragranced the air, or at least some home
with its familiarities lingering on the tip of leaves
and rain. For a moment, I felt disoriented, like when light
first strikes closed eyes.

6

How old am I again?

7

Do the long-haired bands still croon love ballads and hump
guitars?

8

The heat here blisters, and there it is worse—
I'm sure—
with dust and dogs seeking shade under
the bodhi tree whose branches are heavy
as afternoon storm clouds.

9

Buddha says a disconnected family is a storm that plays
havoc in the garden.

10

Buddha left his family to become Buddha.

11

You left to return to heated happiness.

12

No happiness is gained without sacrifice. Without severing.

13

The both of us pick at scabs over our chests, though we relay nothing
to each other of our loneliness
deep

14

in the earth.

15

What if what we grow still dies?
Grow nothing then. Leave earth barren,
but pluck the weeds that seek to suffocate. It's easy
to let them take over, and soon, they will devour
the house, and the lives within the house, and soon,
there will be no home to speak of, no trace
that we were ever alive

16

and in this world.

Beautiful Sadness

—for Katie

My love, you have a face that belies truth,
and I can't figure out
by the red splotches on your cheeks whether you are hot
or have been suffering again
over the losses
of your younger life, those resonating pains
like a child stuck in a bramble of blackberry thorns.

There are moments I catch you
by the window overlooking the Florida flat,
hand pressed against glass, and a cardinal streaks
to the leafy shade of an oak. How I wish
I can catch him, and lay his fervent body in your palms,
a thing determined for flight, and the wind
from those beating wings would blow
away the shadows in your heart.
I believe, my love, this bird can save you, us,
from the storms clouding
the horizon. Press him to your chest,
then let him go.

The World Drowns Atlas

Some days I count the ways the world
has escaped me. Some days the number extends
beyond the limits of my fingers and toes. Some days,
good days,
I can think of only one.

I can't ſtop the world.

It has its own thing
going, and slowing
its rotation for my pleasure
is not one of them. Not even when a hummingbird
sips hibiscus, not even when it buzzes
in bravado. This is what I want
slowed, this moment, so I'm able to decipher
which wing flits faſter, so I can surmise
whether the hummingbird opens it's beak
to speak.

There are other moments, too. Like that afternoon,
when my mother boarded a plane to go away
from America,
away and away.
If I had a longer second to survey her face
for hesitation
on her brow, her lips, her eyes,
I might fully underſtand the complexity of her leaving.
Or not.

Buddha speaks of the world and its purpose. Buddha speaks a lot
of things, many of which are convoluted Rubik cubes. But there is wisdom
in confusion, as there are answers in questions.

Atlas, my friend, the world is heavy. Put it down.
Let time sort itself out.

Because the World Is Cluttered

like the back of my car, a graveyard
of water bottles and wet socks, like my tornado-ed
thoughts, debris whirling and whirling, splinters
and nails and ruined homes—

we need that moment Buddha speaks of, the ability
to see the miracle of a single flower, its blossom
like hands praying beyond sky,
praying for stars to plummet into the bloom.

Let that light shine in shadowed places, let it stir
us from our silent slumber.
Remember the heart is biology—
muscle and veins and arteries.

It will bleed if we let it.

Into the Keeping of Men

There walked a woman today, at the grocery
ſtore, who turned the heads of the meat men behind
refrigerated ſteaks. How they devoured
her elegant ſtride. How her presence was body
without mind. They will remember her—only
briefly—as the one with long legs, the one with gracious
hips, and she will be catalogued
away with infinite others, a forever liſt
of parts.

Giorgione, when you painted Venus, reclined,
her hand seduĉtively positioned above her groin,
what dreams did you give her? Did you fill
her head with the scent of olives and Tuscan
suns? Does painter and subjeĉt occupy
the same breath?

My wife sits alone
in her room, the night air
laden with grief,
a guitar on her lap. How do I paint
her voice and the sound of pluck chords? How do I
capture the beating within her cheſt,
the sad song singing in her heart?

I am learning to see.
Firſt, I close my eyes.

In Thailand It Is Night

Today, my mother dreams of the years
she lost, standing like a river queen
on a wobbling canoe, oar digging into the murky

water of the Chaopaya, her five sisters picking
ticks from her toes. She is thirty-two
and not a nurse in a far away country, not

married to a man who loves to suck
the skin off a stewed chicken's feet, not
giving birth in the early morning,

the sun rising over a lake that roars
like an ocean. No, in her dream
she chooses which way the canoe floats.

In the distance, on the east bank,
a boy holds the sweetest mango, pulp
pale, juices running down the lengths

of his offering arms. But she drifts past,
heads for the red mountains of the north,
the place that has called to her for years.

When she wakes, she calls her only son
and tells him of her dream.
It is time to go home.

The sun has gotten too bright,
and she yearns for those hot nights
when geckos claw up screened windows,

and dogs tumble in the dusty road,
howl at the bitten moon.

HANUMAN

(God-king of the Apes)

What I Want to Remember in the Next Life

That each morning begins with birds.

That spring evenings wake tree frogs into chirping frenzies; that their sound is the metronymic beat of your sleep; that you enter symphonic dreams of crescendo croaking.

That the beagle next door bays to be let in; that it loves its little girl to the point of squeals; that this love is limitless.

That once you were a boy and did boy things and your father and his callused hand touched the back of your bare neck and squeezed, and it felt like he was passing all he had into you, all his other lives, all his other sorrows, and when his hand left what remained was its phantom warmth.

That once you rolled out of a moving car with a doughnut in your mouth; that the accident was so quick you didn't stop chewing.

That your dog brings her velvet head under your hand, even when you are despondent because the world has broken its promises.

That the green before the storm is the quietest time on earth.

That the swallowtail kites fly linguistic patterns in the open sky; that they arrive once a year with an invisible message; that this message is as mysterious as a geode.

That Buddha was a lost prince before he became Buddha; that his story has a beginning and an end and a beginning.

That time never moves backwards but memory does and what was lost could be found again; that if you whisper remember, remember, you will find what it is you are looking for, like the gecko that clings desperately to the tree in a storm, trusting it won't blow away but climb from this life to the next and to the next.

Acknowledgments

Grateful acknowledgment is made to the following publications in which some of these poems appeared, some in slightly different versions:

Blood Lotus: "Fortune"
Buddhist Poetry Review: "Because the World Is Cluttered"
Cha: An Asian Literary Magazine: "Crossing the River Kwai."
Georgetown Review: "How To Tell Your Mother There Will Be No Grandkids In Her Future"
Mead: The Magazine of Literature and Libations: "Into the Keeping of Men""
Mipoesia: "An Attempt to Explain Reincarnation" and "The Country I Never Had"
Naugatuck River Review: "My Father's Life In Six Stanzas"
Ninth Letter: "In Thailand it is Night"
River Styx: "Karma"
Salt Hill: "Ill Man Bowling Alley"
Slant: "Third World Dogs"
Tigertauk: "Bird Dreaming"
Witness: "After the First Snow" and "When Peacocks Scream"

"In Thailand it is Night" also appeared in *Best New Poets 2005*.
"When Peacocks Scream" also appeared in *We the Creatures* (C.J. Sage editor, Dream Horse Press).

About the Author

IRA SUKRUNGRUANG is the author of the memoir *Talk Thai: The Adventures of Buddhist Boy* and the coeditor of two anthologies on the topic of obesity: *What Are You Looking At? The First Fat Fiction Anthology* and *Scoot Over, Skinny: The Fat Nonfiction Anthology*. He is the recipient of the New York Foundation for the Arts Fellowship in Nonfiction Literature, an Arts and Letters Fellowship, and the Emerging Writer Fellowship. His work has appeared in many literary journals, including *Post Road*, *The Sun*, and *Creative Nonfiction*. He is one of the founding editors of *Sweet: A Literary Confection* (sweetlit.com), and teaches in the MFA program at University of South Florida. For more information about him, please visit: www.sukrungruang.com.

About the Book

In Thailand It Is Night is set in Deepdene, designed by Frederic Goudy and named for his home and studio in Marlboro, New York, where he designed it. Goudy cut the matrices and made the types originally for his own use, first employing them for a book of poetry, *Two Singers,* by Charles Hanson Towne, that Goudy set and printed in his shop with the help of Peter Beilenson, who later established the Peter Pauper Press. Goudy's roman and italic designs were adapted for digital types in the Lanston Type Collection from the P22 Type Foundry in Buffalo, New York. The book was designed and typeset by Richard Mathews at the University of Tampa Press. It has been printed on acid-free paper in support of the Green Press Initiative.

POETRY FROM THE UNIVERSITY OF TAMPA PRESS

John Blair, *The Occasions of Paradise**

Jenny Browne, *At Once*

Jenny Browne, *The Second Reason*

Christopher Buckley, *Rolling the Bones**

Christopher Buckley, *White Shirt*

Richard Chess, *Chair in the Desert*

Richard Chess, *Tekiah*

Richard Chess, *Third Temple*

Kevin Jeffery Clarke, *The Movie of Us*

Jane Ellen Glasser, *Light Persists**

Benjamin S. Grossberg, *Sweet Core Orchard**

Dennis Hinrichsen, *Rip-tooth**

Kathleen Jesme, *Fire Eater*

Steve Kowit, *The First Noble Truth**

Lance Larsen, *Backyard Alchemy*

Lance Larsen, *Genius Loci*

Lance Larsen, *In All Their Animal Brilliance**

Julia B. Levine, *Ask**

Julia B. Levine, *Ditch-tender*

Sarah Maclay, *Whore**

Sarah Maclay, *The White Bride*

Sarah Maclay, *Music for the Black Room*

Peter Meinke, *Lines from Neuchâtel*

John Willis Menard, *Lays in Summer Lands*

Kent Shaw, *Calenture**

Barry Silesky, *This Disease*

Jordan Smith, *For Appearances**

Jordan Smith, *The Names of Things Are Leaving*

Jordan Smith, *The Light in the Film*

Lisa M. Steinman, *Carslaw's Sequences*

Marjorie Stelmach, *Bent upon Light*

Marjorie Stelmach, *A History of Disappearance*

Ira Sukrungruang, *In Thailand It Is Night*◊

Richard Terrill, *Coming Late to Rachmaninoff*

Richard Terrill, *Almost Dark*

Matt Yurdana, *Public Gestures*

* Denotes winner of the Tampa Review Prize for Poetry

◊ Denotes winner of the Anita Claire Scharf Award